Grandfather
By Another Name

Grandfather By Another Name

ENDEARING STORIES ABOUT WHAT
WE CALL OUR GRANDFATHERS

Carolyn J. Booth and Mindy B. Henderson

RUTLEDGE HILL PRESS®

Nashville, Tennessee

Copyright © 1998 by Carolyn J. Booth and Mindy B. Henderson

Photographs on pages 17 and 46 © by Jean-Claude Lejeune and used by permission. Photograph on p. 64 © by Alden A. Lockridge and used by permission. Photographs on page 107 © 1994 and page 110 © 1991 by Bob Schatz and used by permission. All other photographs courtesy of the authors.

Poems on pages 38 and 115 written by the author, Mindy Henderson, as a child.

Story on page 71 is reprinted with permission from "Grandfathers Watch" in *Gifts of Our Fathers* edited by Thomas R. Verny. © 1994 Thomas R. Verny. Published by The Crossing Press: Freedom, CA.

Published by Rutledge Hill Press®, 211 Seventh Avenue North, Nashville, Tennessee 37219. Distributed in Canada by H. B. Fenn & Company, Ltd., 34 Nixon Road, Bolton, Ontario L7E 1W2. Distributed in Australia by The Five Mile Press Pty, Ltd., 22 Summit Road, Noble Park, Victoria 3174. Distributed in New Zealand by Tandem Press, 2 Rugby Road, Birkenhead, Auckland 10. Distributed in the United Kingdom by Verulam Publishing, Ltd., 152a Park Street Lane, Park Street, St. Albans, Hertfordshire AL2 2AU.

Typography by Compass Communications, Inc., Nashville, Tennessee
Design by Harriette Bateman
Jacket photograph by Robert Pierce

Library of Congress Cataloging-in-Publication Data

Booth, Carolyn J., 1938—
    Grandfather by another name : enduring stories about what we call our grandfathers / Carolyn J. Booth and Mindy B. Henderson.
        p.   cm.
    ISBN 1-55853-593-4 (hardbound)
    1. Grandfathers.   2. Nicknames.   3. Grandparent and child.
I. Henderson, Mindy B., 1960–   . II. Title.
HQ759.9.B667   1998
306.874'5—dc21   98-11052
                                                                              CIP

Printed in the United States of America
1 2 3 4 5 6 7 8 9 — 02 01 00 99 98

This book is dedicated to

David Holland Booth and Edward Lee Henderson,
the most loving supportive grandfathers in the world
to my children, Jared and Jessica.
God has blessed my family with
these two wonderful men.

I also dedicate this book to
the memory of my grandfathers,
Dudley Howard Booth and John Wilburn Jenkins,
who raised the wonderful children
that became my parents.

Mindy

Foreword

My father, Mindy's Granddaddy Jenkins, greatly loved his large family. Mindy and her sisters were not priviledged to be a part of their granddaddy's life, but his spirit, love, and family values are definitely very much a part of them. He instilled in all of us the importance of respect, loyalty, and unconditional love. The whole family, not just those living under one roof, but aunts, uncles, and cousins—he'd call them "your kin folks"—was important to him too.

This, more than monetary riches, was his legacy to be passed on from his children to their children. It continues now to a fourth generation and, yes, generations to come.

Close families beget happy people, and happy people make the world better. Eighty-five happy people, Granddaddy Jenkins's children, grandchildren, and great-grandchildren, celebrated Christmas together this year. He taught us well. Oh! How he would have smiled to see us all together.

If you have a grandfather, visit him. Spend time listening and talking with him. Call him, write to him, give him a hug, and tell him how very much you love him. Do it today—you'll be glad you did!

If you are a grandfather, give your grandchildren what they long for most—your time. Read to them, rock and sing to them, play with them, attend their special activities, encourage them, listen and talk to them, teach them to pray and to know God. The greatest inheritance you can leave them is a part of your heart given with time and unconditional love, *because grandfathers are special by any name!*

Carolyn

Acknowledgments

Many thanks go out to our families and friends
who have supported us throughout the process of
writing this book. Special thanks to
Larry Stone, Peaches Scribner, and Bryan Curtis.
Your support and encouragement helped
us make our dream come true!

A Grandfather's Perspective

The sweetest sound to the ears of a grandfather is the endearing name his grandchildren give him. It not only conveys recognition but also a depth of feeling expressed in no other way.

To four of my grandchildren I am Paw Paw, but two others call me Pawp. After I am gone, the cherished memories they associate with those names will long remain. Remnants of those memories will be passed on to generations yet unborn, all because that special name was given to me by my precious grandchildren.

A glimpse of such a legacy in the future is deeply sobering. The mental image of a loving grandfather may be a piece of the picture that his grandchildren carry to maturity as a part of their concept of godliness. What an opportunity! What a gift! What a responsibility! Oh, that I can make a difference, an eternal difference, in the lives of children.

To all grandfathers, your special name is yours to wear and fashion into its own treasured feeling in the eternal spirits of your grandchildren.

David Booth

Grandfather
By Another Name

King

MY FATHER has always called me his little princess. He is a very sweet and kind man who loves to give big hugs. I remember many times when he would come home from work and sit in his big lounge chair. I would sit in his lap, and he would say, "How was your day, Princess?" I always knew I was very special to him.

The years passed so fast. It wasn't long until I was married and had a very active little girl of my own. My father was so delighted when my daughter was born. He calls her his "little angel." He was very careful not to call her Princess—after all, that title belonged to me!

My daughter called him Granddaddy up until the time she was six years old. I'll never forget the night when we were at my parents' house for dinner. Daddy was sitting in his lounge chair and my daughter was sitting on the floor playing. As I walked into the room he motioned for me to sit in his lap. I sat down and hugged his neck. "How are you doing, Princess?" he asked. My daughter had heard him call me this before, but she had never said anything. It was as if she had heard it for the first time. She stopped playing and looked at my father.

"Granddaddy, why do you call my mommy Princess?" she asked.

"Because she's my little princess" he answered. "Do you know that no matter how old your mommy gets she will always be my princess?"

"Well," said my very astute six-year-old, "if she is your princess that must mean that you are a king and Grandmommy is the queen!"

We laughed at that. "I guess you're right" he said. That is the night we started calling Granddaddy and Grandmommy King and Queen.

One night as my father and I were standing in the kitchen watching my daughter and her new baby brother playing together, he put his arm around me, leaned over, and whispered, "I may not be as monetarily rich as a king, but oh, look at the riches I have." I hugged him so tight! He is definitely royalty in all of our sights.

Cool Pop

JOSH'S STEP-GRANDFATHER had no children of his own. When he married Josh's grandmother, he inherited an entire family, and he was very excited. He took to Josh with all the fervor of a true, blooded grandfather. He and Josh go fishing and play ball, and he makes special phone calls to Josh just to see how school is going and how he is doing.

Whenever Josh visits, his step-grandfather always has Josh's favorite treat waiting for him—a frozen ice cool-pop. From that came the perfect name for the coolest grandfather—Cool Pop!

{The Wisest Thing My Grandfather Ever Said Was . . .}

Be thankful for what you have.

Boy-Boy

WHEN JOHN Perrin married my husband's mom, she lovingly nicknamed him John-Boy. When our son Tyler began talking and naming his grandparents, we all tried to get him to call his step-grandfather John-Boy. Tyler decided to call him Boy-Boy instead. The name just stuck. Tyler was going to call his grandparents what he wanted regardless of what we wanted them to be called! Even though Tyler is now old enough to say John-Boy, he still says Boy-Boy.

Tyler and his Boy-Boy have the best time together. I think Tyler keeps John-Boy young, and John-Boy certainly makes Tyler feel big.

I Love My Grandfather Because . . .

He rides me on his lawn mower.

Daddoo

ONE SUMMER my family—my dad, my stepmother, and my stepsister—went to Sea World. I was six or seven years old. It was one of the earliest recollections that I have of spending time with my new stepmother and stepsister.

When we returned from our vacation, my parents started asking what I wanted to call my new step-grandparents. At first I wanted to call my step-grandmother Shamu because I had been so impressed with the whale at Sea World. My dad, for obvious reasons, did not believe she would like that name. Therefore I decided to call her Mamoo, because it rhymed with Shamu.

That's when I decided to make things easy. For my step-grandfather, I figured if I had a name that rhymed with Mamoo, that would make his name easy to remember. So I called him Daddoo. Mamoo and Daddoo.

Daddoo is so cool and fun. He calls me every holiday and sings to me. For instance, every year on Christmas he calls and sings, "Here comes Santa Claus, here comes Santa Claus, right down Easter Bunny Lane." Daddoo is also very smart. He is handicapped. He invented a hunting gun for handicapped people that is light and is made for people who only have the use of one hand.

The best thing about my Daddoo is that you would never know that I am his *step*-granddaughter. He treats me so great. I love him very much.

George Bush, State of the Union Address, 1990

"I'm going to ask something of every one of you. Let me start with my generation, the grandparents out there. You are our living link to the past. Tell your grandchildren the story of the struggles waged, at home and abroad; of sacrifices freely made for freedom's sake. And tell them your own story as well—because every American has a story to tell."

Famous Grandfathers and Grandchildren

N. C. Wyeth and James Wyeth
Both grandfather and grandson were famous American artists.

Methuselah and Noah
Methuselah was the oldest man in the Bible, and his grandson Noah steered the ark.

William Henry Harrison and Benjamin Harrison
William was the 9th president of the United States and Benjamin was the 23rd.

Oscar Hammerstein and Oscar Hammerstein
The elder Hammerstein was a well–known German–American operatic impresario who built the Harlem Opera House and the Manhatten Opera House. The younger Hammerstein is one of the most famous American lyricists and librettists. He collaborated on some of the most memorable musicals such as *The Sound of Music* and *Oklahoma*.

Erasmus Darwin and Charles Darwin
Erasmus Darwin wrote a long poem called *The Botanic Garden,* which expounded the Linnaean system. His poem *Zoonomia* explained organic life in evolutionary terms. Charles Darwin developed the theory of organic evolution.

DeDaddy

WHEN MY aunts and uncles began to have children, the kids called my grandfather Granddaddy or Daddy Ganus. Then my brother Dickie came along. He was just learning to talk and he would climb up in my grandfather's lap and say, "DeDaddy."

Well, my MeMaw did not like this one little bit! She kept persuading Dickie to call his grandfather Granddaddy. Soon, Dickie was saying, "GeeDeDaddy." The "GeeDe" didn't sound very nice at all, so, reluctantly, my MeMaw agreed that DeDaddy would do. After some time, every one agreed it was a very cute name.

My sweet DeDaddy was the funniest man I ever knew. He would play tricks on us all the time; he loved to hear us laugh! He was also very wise. I was always impressed that he had read through every version of the Bible many times. DeDaddy was **de**dicated to his family, **de**lightful to be around, and **de**ar to my heart.

MD

MY FATHER is a Ph.D. and a lovable eccentric. When my husband and I were dating, he would come to my house to pick me up and find my father on our roof. Dad was reroofing at the time. Dad would yell down a greeting to my husband and actually carry on conversations with him from the roof.

My husband was so amused by this white-bearded professor and their rooftop chats that he immediately began calling him the Mad Doctor to all of his friends. The name eventually leaked out, and luckily, my father was a good sport about it. I mean, he *did* let me marry the guy. Over the years Mad Doctor was shortened to MD. Sixteen years later, my children, Lee, age nine, and Dawson, age five, love calling him MD and get a bigger kick out of hearing the story!

G-Daddy

WHEN I was asked to tell why I call my grandfather G-Daddy, I had to stop and think. Obviously, it is short for Granddaddy, but another thought occurred to me. Maybe it is because he is good-looking, gallant, good-hearted, and gracious. Or maybe it is because he is gentle, generous, and giving. Any one of these could fit my grandfather. He is the greatest!

The righteous man leads a blameless life; blessed are his children after him.

—Proverbs 20:7

MiMiDaddy

A MAN IS blessed when he lives in a house with three females—two daughters and a wife who shower him with love and attention. I am that man! Add yet another blessing—my first grandchild, a beautiful granddaughter.

However, I realized soon after Camille was born that a granddaughter and grandmother have a special bond. Camille's MiMi was the first to get a smile, her little arms reached first for MiMi, and her cries to stay with MiMi were evidence of her love for her MiMi. It was when she began to call me MiMiDaddy (because I was the daddy at MiMi's house) that I realized things were changing. I clearly took second place to MiMi in Camille's eyes. I accepted this and was just happy she recognized that her MiMi and I belonged together, because, you see, I love her MiMi, too, and she has always been first in my heart!

When our grandson Clark was born, I was excited to have a boy around. Being a fisherman, I began to play and dream about how we would camp and fish together. Somehow in my mind I could not see Clark calling his fishing buddy MiMiDaddy. I

promptly began to call myself Granddaddy to him. He is three now, and yes, he calls me Granddaddy, but if Camille wants to call me MiMiDaddy—well, I guess I'll answer to that too!

Duke

MY NAME is Floyd "Duke" Barrett. Sixty years ago Dr. R. S. Duke delivered me, and my mother nicknamed me for the doctor.

When our son and his wife were expecting our first grandchild, they decided they wanted me to be Daddy Duke. Indeed, our granddaughter Christy called me Daddy Duke until she was about two. Then one day she looked at me with those big brown eyes and said, "You used to be Daddy Duke, and now you're just Duke."

Now Christy has a brother, Will, and he also calls me Duke.

I never miss a ball game or any event that my grandchildren participate in. Their NaNa and I support them in everything they do. We love those two children with a passion. Well we should—because even though they call me Duke, they make me feel like a King.

Tootie

A S A YOUNG man, my maternal grandfather built a train in the backyard of the family home. This train later ended up at Elitch Gardens, an amusement park in Denver.

Of course, when my little brother was born, my grandfather gave him a toy train. Whenever my brother was playing with the train, my grandfather would come around the corner with another train and say, "Toot! Toot! Toot Toot!" So we started calling him Tootie.

My Tootie was the kind of grandfather you could truly talk with; we would have long conversations. He and my grandmother, Mumsie, told us many family stories and created memories we will hang on to for the rest of our lives. We could see when they looked into our eyes that they were so proud of us.

My favorite recollection of Tootie was when I went to stay at their house when I was a junior in high school. I had just started dating, and my date came to pick me up at Mumsie and Tootie's house. They told me to be in by midnight. I set my grandmother's alarm clock on "slow" so that the time on the clock didn't really move every second. She didn't know I did this—or so I thought. I didn't come in until 2:00 in the morning. As I walked in the front door, I saw Tootie sitting in his chair in the living room. I was doomed!

We had a heart-to-heart chat. He told me how worried he and Mumsie had been and that if I was going to be late I should have called and that, oh, by the way, the slow speed on the clock didn't work.

I went to bed feeling terribly guilty and dreading the next day. I just knew I'd be in big trouble when Mom and Dad got home. Mumsie and Tootie never told Mom and Dad about that night, at least not until many years later.

It taught me a lesson about honesty and consideration I'll never forget. "If you're running late, someone who cares about you is waiting. *Call!* Don't make that person worry for no reason." That was the point my grandfather wanted to make. He loved me that much. And oh, how I loved him!

{The Wisest Thing My Grandfather Ever Said Was . . .}

It does not matter what color you are,
we are all the same in God's eyes.

~

You can never love someone you haven't laughed with.

~

Don't ever turn down anything that's free.

~

Stay away from fire ants.

~

Treat others the way you want to be treated.

Ogre

WHEN I was in high school I was an average teenager, but my father was very strict. When it came to curfews, friends, boyfriends, school, whatever, he always made it very clear to me that it was "his way or the highway."

One night when I had missed my curfew, he was waiting at the door for me. We got into a huge fight, and finally I yelled out, "You are just a big ogre!" Well, guess what. That name stuck!

Now that he is a grandfather and has matured and aged—*he has not changed a bit!* He is still set in his ways and very stubborn, and when someone makes him mad I'm pretty sure his eyes glow red—just like an ogre!

All of his grandchildren call him Ogre. He loves us all very much and we all love him, and he thinks the name Ogre is funny. We still think he carries all of the characteristics associated with the name. I guess he's a lovable Ogre—if there is such a thing!

Big Buddy

FROM THE minute I first laid eyes on my grandson, he and I have had a very strong bond; I've always called him my little buddy. One day we were spending our special time together, and I called him Little Buddy. He looked up and smiled at me and called me Big Buddy. He had figured that out all by himself! I was so proud of my smart grandson!

He is now nine and has a brother who is five. We go on hikes and fishing trips, go to ball games, and spend as much time together as we can. We are all best friends—and best buddies.

I Love My Grandfather Because . . .

He lathers me up and lets me "play shave" with him.

Granddaddy Bro

MR. WILLIAM is a concierge at a hotel in Knoxville. He is the father of five, the grandfather of four, and the great-grandfather of one.

He has always been the type to lend a hand or an ear to anyone in need of help. He worked at a hospital for thirty years, drives the church van, takes care of his invalid wife, and now works at the hotel. He always, always has a smile.

When he was growing up, everyone called him Bro. It was an endearing term, an expression of affection. When his first son was born, the boy picked up on the name and called him Bro instead of Daddy. All of the children followed that lead. So, of course, when his grandchildren were born, they called him Grandaddy Bro.

Grandaddy Bro wakes up every day and thanks God for the wonderful life he has. It is certain that his family does the same-except we're sure that each day they also thank God for a wonderful man like Grandaddy Bro.

Top Ten Names for Grandfathers

1. Granddaddy

2. Grandpa

3. PaPa

4. Paw Paw

5. Granddad

6. Grandfather

7. Pop

8. Daddy _____(first or last name)

9. Paw

10. Granddaddy _____(first or last name)

Duck

W HEN BETH was little, her granddaddy would make her laugh by using his Donald Duck voice. As she began to talk, she would hurriedly make her way through the house, run to her granddaddy, and say "Do a duck! Do a duck!"

As Beth grew older, she shortened the request simply to "Duck," and her granddaddy adopted that as his grandfather name. All of the grandchildren call him Duck now. He may not be a Donald, but he sure sounds like him, and he is every bit as much fun!

I Love My Grandfather Because . . .

He wrote me notes when I was in college.

BoBo Sam

WHEN MY ex-husband, Sam, was younger, all of his friends would tease him and call him Sambo. He hated that nickname! So, whenever we wanted to tease him we would call him Sambo.

When my grandson Tony was born, my son thought it would be funny to have Tony call his grandfather Sambo. Sam, on the other hand, wanted to be called Granddaddy or PawPaw, but Tony would have none of it. He insisted on calling his grandfather BoBo Sam.

The first time he called Sam this we all laughed hysterically. Every time he would say "BoBo Sam" he would squint his little eyes at us as if to say "OK, when are you going to laugh?"

Sam is BoBo Sam only to Tony. The other grandchildren don't call him that, so it is a special nickname. Well, Sam did get away from being called Sambo—at least in a way!

Tar

MY FATHER-IN-LAW has always been a man with a heart for children. His years as a high school headmaster have given him much experience communicating with older children, so I imagine when he became a grandfather four times in a span of a little more than a year he was quite overwhelmed with how to deal with these smaller creatures.

He wasn't the least bit worried about what they would call him but more with how to entertain them. Consequently, my mother-in-law, BB, decided because of his cuddly demeanor and lovable personality the kids could call him Bear.

As the first four became old enough to really crawl and play he would pull down his guitar and play for the babies and sing or let them sit on his lap and pluck on the strings.

When my son started to talk he would go right in the house to my father-in-law and say "Tar!" and point to the wall where the guitar hung. Amazingly, the others, who were also on the verge of talking, followed suit and would also call for their "Tar." Despite many efforts on the part of BB and the aunts to come up

with a more suitable grandfather name, the babies refused to call their beloved grandfather anything but Tar. I think it only appropriate that a man with such a heart was given a name that really means nothing but signifies a love communicated to the hearts of babies.

My Grandfather

My grandfather is so big and tall
You hardly notice his wrinkles at all.
He has three corns on each of his toes
And he wears wire glasses on his nose.

He has shoes that are three sizes too big
And in his middle he looks like a pig.
He makes me laugh, he makes me giggle
When with the hoola, he does a wiggle.

He wears his overalls all the time
And sings funny songs that never rhyme.
He's a horrible cook, and I hate to say
He doesn't cook good any day.

I don't care about how he looks;
I don't care about how he cooks.
I love my grandfather, he's like no other,
And best of all he's married to my grandmother!

CowPa

MUCH TO my paternal grandfather's chagrin, I took the name he had hoped I would call him, Grandpa, and gave it a creative twist of my own. My grandparents lived on a farm on the outskirts of a small community. Their farm had all the trappings of the *Fun at the Farm* books my mother read to me at night—a big red barn stacked with sweet-smelling hay, typical farm equipment, a garden filled with delicious country vegetables that would be canned for the winter, and of course, cows!

Sometimes my grandfather would lock the tractor's blade in the upright position and let me drive around the pasture, surveying the crops and stock. No one knows exactly why, but after one of our trips, I came back to the house calling him CowPa instead of Grandpa.

Neither he nor Grandma was thrilled with the nickname I had chosen. After listening to them for a little bit, I told them they were very fortunate that I had not taken my association of Grandpa and the cows one step further—to CowPaddy. They laughed and agreed—so to this day I lovingly call him CowPa.

Hot Dog

O F ALL their seven grandchildren, my nephew Tyler was the one my parents spent the least amount of time with. When he spent a week with them one summer he had not decided what to call them. (They're Nana and Granddaddy to all of the other grandchildren.)

So Mom and Daddy were suggesting all the old standards like Granddad, Pop Pop, Paw Paw, and Tyler kept saying a strong "no" to everything they brought up. Finally, I guess my mother was a little weary of going through all the names, and as she got tired, she got a little silly. When she offered Hot Dog to Tyler as a name for my dad, he lit right up and said, "That's it!" Now, my dad is the most humble, soft-spoken, sweet man you would ever meet. He is not at all the show off that the name Hot Dog connotes, but to Tyler he is a very special Hot Dog indeed.

Happy

SULLIE IS the eternal optimist. He can take a gray day and make it bright. He is joyful and always happy!

When he and his wife, Carolyn, found out they were going to be grandparents for the first time, Sullie excitedly took to the idea with great delight and began to tease Carolyn, saying, "We'll be Granny and Pappy!"

Later, enjoying every moment with his beautiful new granddaughter Leigh, he would always say, "Come to your old pappy."

Whether Leigh couldn't say "pappy" or whether she picked up on her grandfather's cheerful nature, when she began to talk she called him Happy.

Now, years later, Leigh and the other five grandchildren all call him Happy. Everybody's happy when Happy's around!

{The Wisest Thing My Grandfather Ever Said Was . . .}

If you show respect, you will get respect.

Daddy Bob

I CALL my grandfather Daddy Bob. His real name is Robert Overton. To some, Daddy Bob might seem like a common grandfather name for anyone named Bob or Robert. It's a name I'm proud of because I am named Robert after him, and I think he is an extraordinary grandfather, very far from common.

After Daddy Bob retired, he moved to Colorado. When I was in junior high, I looked forward to visiting him on summer breaks, because he did so many cool things that boys love to do. For instance, he and a couple of other men decided to build a church in the small town where they lived. They didn't contract it out. They built it with their own hands. He put me to work on it too. When it was finished, I was proud to be able to worship in a building I had helped my grandfather and his friends build.

He was also an outdoorsman. He taught me to fish. We had great conversations, and I grew very close to him in those times. He also taught me how to camp. I remember his telling me to store the eggs and bacon away from the camp, because that's what the bears would be looking for. That really added a sense of excitement to the trip! When it snowed, he taught me how to ride a snowmobile over the Colorado land. I loved doing all of these things with him—and still enjoy them now as an adult.

One of my fondest memories is of Daddy Bob teaching me how to be a salesman. My cousin and I were visiting him one summer. He bought us a cherry orchard, and we picked cherries all day. (He paid us one dollar an hour). When it came time to sell them, we took the "fruits" of our labor to a local Native–American reservation. I was nervous about selling our baskets of cherries, but Daddy Bob advised me to let my customers sample the cherries. I did, and before we knew it we had sold them all! We took the money, and the three of us went to eat a big steak dinner that night.

I love him for his wisdom, his guidance, and his love of God and others. I just love *him* very much, and I am proud to carry his name.

I Love My Grandfather Because . . .

He made me a tree swing.

Ray Ray

MY GRANDFATHER was named Raymond, and so was my father. Once, when my dad and grandfather visited a church in La Porte, Indiana, the pastor of the church introduced my father to his daughter. "This is Raymond," he said. Then he turned to my grandfather and said to the little girl, "And this is Raymond."

"Oh! More Ray Ray!" she exclaimed.

That is how my grandfather came to be called Ray Ray.

My cousin Chris and I used to spend the night with Ray Ray and our grandmother, Mae Mae. We got a little mischievous one night and decided that after they were in bed we would taste a little drink from each bottle in their liquor closet.

The next morning, we both came downstairs looking a little green around the gills. Ray Ray looked point-blank at us and asked if we needed a drink. We had been caught! We were both so embarrassed. How did he know? We were nervous that he would tell on us. He never told our parents though. From that experience we both learned a lesson we'll never forget! In fact, we learned *two* lessons: that Ray Ray was kind enough not to get us in trouble . . . and that he knew everything! We never tried to pull anything over on him again.

Ray Ray was a kind, loving, grandfather—the very best I could have asked for.

A little boy is busily and laboriously helping his grandfather wash the car. Soon, one of his grandfather's friends comes upon the two working together on the car.

"What's he paying you to help him?" the man asked the young grandson.

"Attention," the boy beamed.

CT

MY CHILDREN'S paternal grandfather, Pop Pop, was a family practice physician. He was a rotund, jovial man—portly with gray hair. We always called him Pop Pop around the children.

When the baby of the family, at around the age of three, started calling him CT, and everyone else just picked it up. We could not figure out why in the world the baby called him CT.

Finally, around Christmas, we were noticing the similarities between Pop Pop and Santa when the answer came to us. Of course! The little one was calling him Santa, and it was coming out CT! The children all called him CT for the next five years, and then he went back to Pop Pop.

How wonderful it must have been to be thought of by his grandchildren as their Santa—jolly, fat (well—maybe), and the bearer of gifts!

Hey Baby

WHEN HIS daughter calls and says she is on the way over with his adorable little granddaughter, this grandfather waits by the door. It might seem unusual for an adult to pace about, waiting for someone to come over. But this little girl is the apple of his eye, the joy of his life.

The car soon pulls into the driveway. Not too proud to let her know he was waiting, he throws open the door. With arms outstretched, he kneels down and waits for what he knows is going to happen.

She is lifted out of her car seat and set down on the asphalt. As she looks toward him a smile covers her face from ear to ear. She runs as fast as her little legs will take her toward her grandfather.

Enveloping her in a big hug, he says, "Hey baby!"

And right back at him she says, "Hey baby!"

It is not only their affectionate greeting but also the special name she calls him: Hey Baby.

Bye-Daddy

MY GRANDMOTHER always called my grandfather Daddy. When he would leave for work or to go out the door, she would wave and say, "'Bye, Daddy!"

Well, as most children do, we grandchildren imitated what we heard her say. We called our grandfather Bye-Daddy.

I love the name so much because it stirs memories of the warmth I could see and feel between my grandparents.

I Love My Grandfather Because . . .

He tells me about different kinds of cows.

I Love My Grandfather Because . . .

He puts me up on his shoulders at the Christmas parade.

He sings silly songs and makes me giggle.

He smells like a pipe.

He taught me to make model airplanes.

He takes me to ball games. We don't sit down—
we walk the fence!

Sneezy

MY HUSBAND has had terrible allergies for as long as I can remember. After a while, I tend to tune out the sniffling and coughing and sneezing.

As luck would have it, our granddaughter was visiting our house one day in the fall when her grandfather's allergies were swinging into high gear. She and I were reading "Snow White and the Seven Dwarfs," and we were really into the story when Granddad started his sneezing. She looked up at me with the sweetest little smile and said, "Nana, I know who Sneezy is!" Then her eyes got big, and she pointed in her grandfather's direction. I burst into laughter! Yes, he was!

My husband, of course, loves to play, and he makes the most of his name. Whenever the grandchildren are around, there is never a small sneeze. He overdoes each one with an "Atchoooooo.....Eeeeeeeee."

They giggle and say, "Sneezy's at it again!"

It has become quite a fun time for us around our house. Thank goodness that Coughy is not one of the seven dwarfs!

Towhead

SOMETIMES, AS a young person, a physical characteristic makes such an impression on family and friends that a nickname is given that stays with the person his or her entire life. Well, that is what happened to my grandfather.

Blessed with flax-colored hair, he became known as Towhead. Now, seventy years later, he is called that by everyone who knows him. In fact, if anyone calls him by his real name, Edward, no one knows who's being talked about.

My Towhead is a wonderfully unique man. Always manly (he is an ex-marine), he barks out orders to us and our grandmother. Even though he can sound so gruff, (and he probably wouldn't want me to say this), I have seen him cry during movies. He has the biggest heart I have ever seen. He is also the best cook I have ever known. He is a real handyman and built me a swing set and shelves. He has also won many golf tournaments in his town. The best thing about him is that he loves me and his other grandchildren so much.

I am proud to say that I am one of three grandchildren with blond hair inherited from him. (His fourth grandchild has brown hair!) I love my Towhead very much and carry his hair color with pride!

Tops

SOMEHOW IT has been a tradition in our family for several generations to call the father Pops. That is what my brother called my father and what my father called my grandfather.

My brother had the first child in our generation, so our parents' first grandchild. When this little boy began to say a few words, for some reason instead of saying Pops it came out Tops. How special it was for a first-time grandfather to be Tops to his first grandchild! Of course, as more grandchildren came along he was also Tops to them too—not only in name but in their hearts.

Tick

DO YOU remember the old song "My Grandfather's Clock"? Well, this special grandfather has an old Pendleton clock that stands in his house. His grandchildren are somewhat awed by the swinging of the pendulum and the striking of the hour, and he picks them up and carries them to watch the clock.

As he is holding them, they stare at the clock in amazement. "Tick-tock, tick-tock," he says. He holds them patiently while the hand moves toward the hour.

His two grandchildren call him Tick. He does, in fact, have many traits in common with the clock: He is steady and faithful. He takes his time, is never in a hurry, and they can always, always count on him. Tick, what a grand grandfather!

The Wisest Thing My Grandfather Ever Said Was . . .

Save your money. Don't spend more than you make.

Do

WHEN DAN Baccus's first grandchild, Sarah, came along, she called him DaDoo. Later her brother, Stan, was born, and when he was old enough to talk, he shortened the name to Do.

Do is a dentist by profession, but he is also an electrician, a plumber, and an all-around handyman. If he comes up against something he does not know how to do, he gets a book and learns how to do it! His family never have to call a repairman for anything.

One day Do had a friend visiting him. Within the course of the visit, a call came that someone had forgotten a bag of groceries at the supermarket. Do left to pick it up. When he returned, he fixed a car radio antenna. After that, someone dropped a contact lens down the drain, and he took the drain apart, retrieved the lens (in good shape!), and put the drain back together. His friend said to him then, "I know why they call you Do! You can *do* anything!"

His friend was right! His name fits him perfectly.

Sugar Sweet

MY GRANDPA'S nickname is Sugar Sweet because he is so, so sweet. He loves me very much, and he acts like a kid. He is so much fun! People say when you grow up you still have a kid's personality in you. My Sugar Sweet sure does!

My mom calls my grandpa a tumble dad. He loves to spoil us. He takes us to see movies and gets us popcorn and candy. He buys us ice cream. We go to his company picnics. (He is a big businessman!) He lets us play on his computer and copy our faces on his color copier!

There is not a sweeter grandpa in the world than my Sugar Sweet. I love him soooooooooooo much!

{The Wisest Thing My Grandfather Ever Said Was . . .}

Keep your bottom in the saddle,
and you won't fall off your horse.

Boo-Daddy

WHEN MY sorority sisters were conducting a late-night discussion on what we called our grandparents, there was no question that Laney's grandfather took the cake for having the most amusing nickname.

When his first grandchild was little, Laney's grandfather loved to sneak up on her and teasingly startle her with a resonating, "BOO!" They played this game all the time, and without fail, his antics sent the child into peals of laughter. Soon, everyone in the house was laughing too.

Laney said her grandfather is very sweet and full of surprises. It did not take long for his grandchildren to begin calling him Boo-Daddy. He's living up to that nickname today for his great-grandchildren too.

Sneak

SNEAK WAS his street name. He was a young, handsome man, a risk taker who ran the streets of Flint, Michigan. His real name was Quinzell White. He was no stranger to life's struggles. He spent the majority of his time trying to make a dollar, selling things he had found and fixed up; he was an entrepreneur of the streets.

He was also a womanizer. He told me he loved to chase the girls (mainly my grandmother, Annette). All of his characteristics helped to give him his nickname. When I was a child I called him Zellie, but as I grew older I called him Sneak too!

As a teenager, I noticed that my grandfather was a very suave gentleman. Even though he was devoted to the Lovely Annette (the name he always called my grandmother), he still had an eye for the ladies. He told me a story once about when he was a younger "player." He took two girls out on the same night to the same place! After the first date was over, he took the first girl home. Five minutes later he picked up another girl and took her to the same restaurant he had just taken the first girl! Little did he know that the first young lady he had just kissed good night was back in the corner of the same restaurant kissing another man! It was at that moment he decided to settle down with Lovely Annette. He adored her until the day he died.

My grandfather shared many other stories with me. Because of his past, he gave me some very wise advice about life and how people can be. If it were not for him I would probably be dead or in trouble right now. I still remember and follow his advice, and I wish he were here to advise me. I loved him, and I miss him very much.

{The Wisest Thing My Grandfather Ever Said Was . . .}

If you don't know where you're going,
you probably won't get there.

PawPaw

WHEN I was born, my brother was already calling my grandfather PawPaw. My PawPaw has three daughters. I was his first granddaughter, and he really took to me because he loves little girls.

I am very possessive of my PawPaw. He calls me Sugar Baby. When my cousin Caroline was born, I heard him call her Sugar Baby too. Well, I set him straight! He could only have one Sugar Baby, and that was me! So he decided to call her Sweet Linegirl.

I don't know why we call him PawPaw. It reminds me of the song "Way Down Yonder in the PaPaw Patch." I know if I were in that papaw patch I would definitely pick my PawPaw and put him in my basket. He's the best grandfather in the universe. I love him very much.

Easy

ISN'T IT funny how we evolve as we grow older? Most young men would never want to be known as Easy. But that is how my father is known to his grandchildren, and he is very proud.

His last name is Eslick. Now, this name lends itself to several nicknames, but my father chose Easy as his grandfather name. My mother, on the other hand, had always liked the name Old Sweet for her grandmother name. When my children and my nephew came along they began calling my mother and father Sweet and Easy. What wonderful, appropriate names for them! They are integral parts of their grandchildren's lives, and they definitely live up to their names.

{The Wisest Thing My Grandfather Ever Said Was . . .}

Don't disagree with a woman.

Cap

MY FATHER and many of his friends often called my grandfather Cap, an unusual name for the man I affectionately knew as Papa. Although I never asked, I assumed that Cap was short for Captain, or maybe, I thought, it meant he was the man in charge. As I grew older, my grandfather proved to be an outstanding leader.

By the time I was ten, I had found out the origin of Cap. During the 1940s and 1950s, the mostly white residents of a small, rural Alabama community rarely discussed the plight of homeless people, much less homeless African Americans. However, Cap, a middle-aged white businessman with an eighth-grade education, did not ignore the needy. He did the unthinkable for that era. He became the guardian (official but not legal) of a young black man named Aubrey.

As if being black, homeless, and living in rural Alabama was not difficult enough, Aubrey also had epilepsy, an incurable and untreatable disease at that time. By most accounts, he would have been considered a social misfit. He felt he had nothing to live for—until he met Cap, the name he gave my grandfather the first time that they met.

For more than twenty years Cap and my grandmother (Aubrey called her Old Miss) provided this poor man with the essentials for a better life: food, money, clothing, shelter, medicine, and most importantly, love, respect, and a feeling of self-worth.

Today, when I see a homeless person, I remember Aubrey and Cap, a most improbable pair of friends. Both now enjoy the good life in heaven. I have often wished I had asked Cap how their relationship began and what bound their friendship, but at the time it didn't seem important. I often dream about the wonderful summer days I enjoyed as a guest in the home of Cap and Old Miss and the fun times I had playing with Aubrey. Those were the times when I learned something about life and a lot about living from a loving grandfather.

Every child should be so fortunate to have a Cap!

{The Wisest Thing My Grandfather Ever Said Was . . .}

Listen to your parents.

PePaw

MY HUSBAND, Donnie, and I did not try to decide what our grandson Cody would call Donnie. We figured he would invent something, and that smart grandson of ours did not let us down.

One day when he was about two years old, I picked up Cody from day care. He loves coming to our house because we spoil him. He also loves our dog, Hootch. As soon as we got in the door, Cody ran through the house, looking for Donnie and Hootch.

"Nana, where's PePaw and Arooch?"

"What?" I asked, laughing because I had never heard these names.

"Where's PePaw and Arooch?" he asked again.

Donnie had taken Hootch for a walk. When he got home, I informed him that his new name was PePaw, and Hootch's new name was Arooch. We got the biggest kick out of this because we had never once said PaPa or Granddaddy or anything to Cody. He just came up with these names on his own. Isn't he mature and smart?

Wink

I HATE to say my grandfather was sneaky, but he was! Never with bad things—always good (at least in my opinion). My grandmother was the rule maker, and he was the rule breaker. I called him Wink.

With each rule he broke, he would look at me with a sparkle in his eye . . . and wink. For instance, my grandmother would say, "No candy before dinner."

"OK" he would respond—and then he would wink at me! As soon as we went into the other room, he would dig two pieces of candy from his pocket, and we would eat them.

He had the cutest grin on his face as he led me into doing all the things my grandmother had told us not to do. Whether it was sneaking sweets, letting me stay up an extra ten minutes beyond the time she had said to go to bed, or letting me roll in the grass when she had told me to keep clean, I always knew I could do these things by that wink he gave me.

One day, however, his wink took on a new meaning. I had had problems at school because some of my friends were speaking badly of another boy that I thought was a good guy. I had taken up for him, and these friends were giving me a really hard time about it. It hurt my feelings, and I decided to talk to Wink about it. He told me I had done the right thing, no matter what the other kids said. He told me to always follow my heart and to do what was right and good. Then he told me he was proud of me! He winked at me and hugged me tight. Even though I was twelve years old, I cried against my grandfather's chest that day.

Now, all these years later, if I sneak around and do some harmless thing like eat something before my wife serves dinner, I smile to myself. More importantly, whenever I stand up for what I believe in, I think of Wink—and know he would still be proud of me.

A good man leaves an inheritance for his children's children.

—PROVERBS 13:22

DooDad

REMEMBER how my spry, cute little grandfather would be fiddling around his garage when I would go to visit. Upon his retirement, he had decided to become a handyman around the house, and he was always doing something: fixing a broken chair, building bookshelves, or repairing a lawnmower.

The funny thing about my grandfather, though, was that he was terrible at this new job he had created for himself! When I would go into the house and ask my grandmother where he was, she would say with exasperation in her voice, "He's out there breaking things!" It was a kind of silent family joke. We would never tell him how horrible he was at being Mr. Fixit.

There were times when I would go out to talk to him while he was working in the garage and he would be looking around for a nut or a bolt or the screwdriver. When I would ask him what he was looking for, he would say, "That little doodad that goes here." He called everything a doodad!

Of course, I picked up on this and began lovingly calling him the DooDad Man. That eventually turned into DooDad. We still fondly think of him today whenever we see something broken around the house. I especially think of him whenever my husband is putting together toys for my children. "Can you hand me that screw, honey?" he asks. "You mean this little doodad?" I answer. DooDad will forever be in my heart.

{The Wisest Thing My Grandfather Ever Said Was . . .}

Don't just take a job for the salary. Check out the benefits.

Teach by example, not by words.

Don't touch a hot surface!

Daddy Green

EVERY LITTLE boy and girl would consider it a dream come true to have a granddaddy with a candy store! For my siblings and me that dream did come true. Our Daddy Green owned a grocery store in Leiper's Fork, Tennessee. The moment we stepped into the store to visit, we would go behind the big counter and get our own big brown paper bag. These bags would then be filled with candy, gum, peanuts, Crackerjacks, and anything else we wanted!

Daddy Green had a special love for all children. A child never left his store without at least a lollipop given to them by our grandfather. Now Green's Grocery is on the Historical Register and has become famous. It gives me such pride to know that that was my grandfather's store. I have wonderful, fond memories of that big, old candy showcase and of my sweet grandfather—whose sweetness surpassed all of the candy in the world.

Grandfather's Watch

The watch, my only palpable connection to my grandfather, is my most treasured possession. When I wear it, I feel more grounded, more complete. Sometimes, in a quiet moment, just before going to sleep, I'll light a candle, darken the room, take out grandfather's watch and hold it in my hands. I am with him again. I am holding on to his hand. It is winter and very cold. The streets are blanketed with snow and there's a stillness in the air, a muffling of street noises that always seems to accompany the arrival of new snow. My grandfather is wearing a long black woolen coat with a fur collar. We are going into a soda pop factory. I am mesmerized by the sight of hundreds of glass bottles passing in front of me on a conveyor belt; siphons fill them with colored liquids. When we finish the tour grandfather buys me a cherry drink. It is a moment full of magic, mystery, wonder and delight. No child ever enjoyed a bottle of pop more than I did. At that moment my grandfather was to me the most awesome and powerful man in the whole world. And I was his grandson. There was nothing the two of us could not do. Together, we were invincible.

Pow Pow

M Y MOTHER had one rule when I was little: "He will not own a toy gun. There will be no play shooting, no army men!" she announced. Well, to my grandfather, that was like saying I had to wear dresses! All little boys play with guns, he argued, whether the game was cowboys and Indians, army, or whatever!

So when he would baby-sit for me, it was our little secret. We would play everything that you could imagine using our thumb and pointer fingers as pretend guns. I would sneak around the corner and shoot him, saying "Pow! Pow!"

"Ugh! You got me!" he would say, grabbing his chest and falling to the floor. From that secret play I began to call him Pow-Pow. My mom always thought it was another version of Paw-Paw, but my grandfather and I knew different. It was a name that brought a smile to his face then—and still does now.

Ikey Pop

I CALL my grandfather Ikey Pop. His real name is Isodore Price Keller, but his nickname has always been Ikey. When I was little, all I ever heard him called was Ikey, so I assumed that was his one-and-only name. I refused to call him Grandpa. When my mother tried to correct me, I wouldn't listen to her.

She tried to get me to call him Grand Pop—which I turned into Ikey Pop. After much frustration on my mother's part, she finally just gave in. I was the first grandchild, so he is now called Ikey Pop by all of the grandchildren. I think it is a wonderful name. I think he is a *wonderful* granddaddy!

I Love My Grandfather Because . . .

He takes me fishing.

Great Ways to Help Your Grandchildren Remember You

- Coach a Little League team.

- Build something together—a birdhouse, model airplane, or a tree house.

- Put on some music and dance together.

- Volunteer at your grandchildren's school to read, tutor, or go on field trips with them.

- Help your grandchildren start a collection you can enjoy together.

- Tell your history over and over in stories.

- Have one-on-one time with each grandchild.

Great Ways to Help Your Grandchildren
Remember You

- Make buying, cutting, or decorating a Christmas tree a tradition you enjoy together.

- Tell your grandchildren about the modern conveniences available now that you didn't have growing up.

- Start a savings account for your grandchildren and add to it on special occasions.

- Take your grandchildren on a trip with you.

- Give your grandchildren something that is special to you, and it will always remind them of you.

- Take a walk, or sit together under a favorite tree and talk.

Pa

EVERYONE IN the small town where my grandparents lived called them Ma and Pa. My Pa was an endearing man, and everyone loved him, but I loved him the most.

Whenever I got to choose a baby-sitter, I would choose Pa. Even though I was terrified of bugs and snakes as a small girl, I loved going with him into the garden on his farm to pick watermelons in the summer and pumpkins in the fall.

He didn't have a lot of money, but he was always looking for reasons to give me a dollar. He would give me money for good report cards. He even gave me a dollar every time I got my hair cut!

The thing I remember most about him, however, is that he treated his six children, fourteen grandchildren, and twenty-four great-grandchildren equally. He had abundant love for his family, and he heaped it upon us until the day he died. I still miss him to this day.

Daddy Slim

MY GRANDFATHER worked building roads and buildings for the state of Alabama. His name was Elihu Harris, and he was very thin.

While he was helping build the post office in the town of Cullman, Alabama, his job was to fill a wheelbarrow with bricks and push it up to the bricklayers. Because of his size the bricklayers doubted he was strong enough to do such a hard job. They also could not remember the name Elihu! So, as he brought each delivery, they would say, "Here comes Slim!" Hence, he took on the name Slim, and later he was called Daddy Slim by all of his grandchildren.

My fondest memory of Daddy Slim is how he would run to our car as soon as we pulled into his driveway. He couldn't wait to see us! He would then load us all into his truck and drive us to the post office to get his mail and then take us to the local Dairy Dip. He loved ice cream and chocolate-covered cherries. He could afford to love these sweets because he was so slim!

Last year my husband and I took the Cullman exit to show our children where their great-grandfather and great-grandmother had lived. We passed the post office he had helped build, and somehow I found, by memory, the house I had visited when I was a little girl. There was something strange about the road to his house, especially considering that he had spent much of his working life building roads. The road was paved all the way up to his address, then there was a section of gravel road in front of his house. Then the pavement resumed after the house.

This visit renewed all my memories of my sweet Daddy Slim. I can't go through a holiday season now without thinking of him every time I see chocolate-covered cherries. Those thoughts lead me to remember again the love and warmth I felt from him.

I Love My Grandfather Because . . .

He loves my grandmother.

He watches ball games on TV with me.

Foreign Grandfather Names

Cheyenne: *Namshim*
Czech: *Ddecek*
Dutch: *Grootvader*
Finish: *Isoisa*
French: *Grand-père*
German: *Opa, Grossvater*
Hawaiian: *Kupuna kāne, Tutu, Kuku*
Hungarian: *Nagyapa*
Icelandic: *Afi*
Italian: *Nonno*
Japanese: *Ojíisan, Sófu*
Norwegian: *Farfar, Morfar, Betefar*
Polish: *Dziadek*
Portuguese: *Avô, Vovô*
Spanish: *Abuelo*
Yiddish: *Zayde*

Popow

PROVERBS 22:16 says, "A good name is more desirable than great riches; to be esteemed is better than silver or gold."

My son Matthew was inadvertently given the opportunity to name his grandparents, Carlos and Linda Reyes, for the next generation of Reyeses. It wasn't long after celebrating his first words that we began to focus on helping him recognize each family member by name. Matthew loved each one of them very much, but he was especially fond of my father, who became his favorite pal.

Attempts at teaching him to say Grandpa, Granddaddy, and even Grandfather were made. He wasn't going for it. No, his enthusiastic choice was and always remained Popow, pronounced Pop-ow.

Nearly fifteen years later, my father is still Popow to Matthew. They continue to be special pals; Matthew deeply loves and respects him. Popow is a good name, worth more than silver and gold to this man who is greatly esteemed by his grandson, (and by two more grandchildren, Meredith and Brandon, as well!)

Baba

MY GRANDFATHER came to America from Ireland when he was fifteen years old. His father, my great-grandfather, brought his family here in search of a better future. He got a job working in a coal mine, and as soon as my grandfather was old enough, he started working there too.

I called my grandfather Baba to set him apart from my other grandparents. My Nana thinks it is a nice variation of the word Grandpa, and I do too. After I was born, my Nana and Baba started calling me Sugar Cookie. My Nana told me that the first thing she ever cooked was sugar cookies, and they were just kind of special to her, just as I was.

My Baba died when I was just four years old. It makes me very sad to know he is gone, but I feel like he is still a very strong part of me.

I Love My Grandfather Because . . .

He built me a tree house.

He is kind, and he always takes up for me.

He helps anyone who needs help.

He is the rock that I cling to in the flood of life—
the only positive male influence in my life.

He is always honest with me.

Paw

MY GRANDFATHER was known in his community as Mr. James (his first name), but we all called him Paw. He was a farmer, a husband, a father of five boys, a grandpa, and a Sunday school teacher at the local Baptist church for most of his adult life.

We took weekend trips to visit Granny T and Paw in Kentucky about once a month. Paw and I would go fishing on one of his ponds or at the river on the edge of his property. I would follow him out to do morning chores and try my best to step into his footprints exactly. (That wasn't so easy to do when Paw was six-foot-three-inches tall and I was barely tall enough to see the middle button on his shirt!) I knew if there was a new calf or pig, I would get to name it and feed it. Paw and I had many long walks and talks. I miss those most of all.

Paw had a language all to himself. He used funny, strange phrases and words, which were interpreted over the years by my dad. One day I heard Paw say we were having "roastneers" for dinner. I was only ten years old and a little worried about what we were going to eat. I finally worked up the nerve to ask my parents after dinner what exactly "roastneers" were, since I had not seen anything on the table that would match that word. They burst into laughter. My dad told me that Paw meant "roasting ears" of corn! This was the best of the crop, set aside from the corn used for hog feed.

Twenty years later, I still try to follow in Paw's big footsteps, and it is still hard. When I become a grandparent myself, I only hope that I can follow his example of being the most loving grandparent God has ever graced the world with.

{The Wisest Thing My Grandfather Ever Said Was . . .}

Don't be overly impressed with people in high places.
They put on their pants one leg at a time, just like you do.

If you dance, you have to pay the fiddler.

Other Names for Grandfather

Anddaddy	DocDoc	PalPal
Ba	Dupes	Pap
Baba	Fat Man	PaPe
Big Dad	G-Daddy	PaPoo
Big Man	Gaddy	PapPap
Big Papa	Gramps	PaWee
BoBo	Gran-Gran	PawPa
BoomPop	Grand _____	Pock
Bop	(first or last name)	PoPa
Bopey	Grandie	Popcie
Buddy	GrandMan	PoPe
DaDa	GrandPal	PoPo
DaDaddy	Grandpee	PoPow
Daddy Kay	Grandpo	Poppie
Daddy 2	Grandy	Sheek
Dado	Granpy	Tadpole
DanDan	Great Dad	TaTa
DeeDee	Mr. Man	TiePaw
DiDad	Opa	Tiger
DigMan	P-Paw	Zaddy

Cupcake

MY GRANDFATHER was a man of some considerable size. This, coupled with his frank manner and his booming voice, could make him quite intimidating. In my childlike innocence, however, I could see his soft and tenderhearted core. I knew he was a very loving and caring man. To me, his size was more endearing than frightening. He reminded me of a teddy bear or of Santa Claus.

Most of all, I secretly thought he looked like a giant cupcake, and that was the nickname I used for him—when he wasn't around. I'm sure as a child I may have slipped and called him that directly, but he never acted like he knew.

There was one thing I did not try to hide, though, and that was my deep affection for him. I would give anything for a big, old Cupcake hug today.

Dada

I CALL my grandfather Dada because I couldn't say Granddaddy when I was little. I probably heard my mom and dad call him Daddy and was trying to say granddaddy, but all I could manage was Dada.

Not many people are fortunate enough to have a grandfather who lives right down the street from them. My Dada lives that close to me, so I can go over to his house anytime I want. I enjoy being around him. He buys me many things, and he takes me many places. Sometimes we even go on vacations with him. I know I can talk to him anytime about anything whenever I need to. He's a great listener, and all he wants in return is a smile and a hug.

He has done so much for me, and I love him a bunch. I am very thankful for my Dada!

I Love My Grandfather Because . . .

He buys tons of my school fund-raising stuff
(even stuff he doesn't need!).

~

He says, "Do good and I'll help you;
do bad and I'll help you more."

~

He says, "Never lose your angel-freckles."

~

He lets me sip his coffee if I promise not to tell my mom.

~

He pretends to be the Beast, and I pretend to be Beauty.

Pooh Bear

SOME GRANDFATHERS get their names by the way they look or act, but we called our grandfather Pooh because that was the only thing we could say when we were little. We added Bear because—well, he told us that he killed a bear. I don't know how he pulled that off or even if I believe it, but they say he did.

Pooh Bear is a get-up-and-go type of character. He never sits around, even at his age, but is always on the go like a teenager. He says he is too cocky and can't rest. (They also say he's been that way ever since he killed the bear, but I don't know about that!) He says, "Life is a competition. You can never rest."

I admire Pooh Bear because he relates to me. Everything I go through, he has been through. His expectations are high for our success, so he is always pushing us to be the best we can be. Once, when we were in a store looking at some toys, he said, "If you want something . . . go get it!" From that time on, he has been my role model.

He is always playing practical jokes on us. He can turn a sad moment into a happy one in the blink of an eye. We have to be careful. We never know when he might surprise us!

If I had to compare him to the storybook Pooh Bear everyone knows, I would say he is always there for us . . . to advise us or tease us or care for us. He is a good friend, and I admire him for being what he is.

Plow Jockey

MY GRANDFATHER is seventy-five years old. He lives in a little town in Michigan that is made up of farmers and small shop owners. When my mom was growing up, he farmed all kinds of crops and had horses and milk cows. Since that time he has retired from farming, but he still lives in the same house in the same town with the same woman, my grandmother, who married him fifty years ago.

As a young boy, I visited my grandfather on my vacation. He would ride a plow and take me along with him. I also used to go to the shed where he stored all of the farming equipment and play on the tractors and plows. He started calling me a plow jockey, so I turned it around and called him one right back! Now it is our special name for each other.

My grandfather means very, very much to me, and sharing this special nickname creates a bond that I appreciate. None of my cousins have this kind of relationship with him.

Plow Jockey is a fair man. He is funny but stern when he has to be. He can always make me laugh. He appreciates every moment. He taught me to have fun and enjoy life! He has always done that. I'll always remember my grandfather as my own Plow Jockey.

I Love My Grandfather Because . . .

He tells me lots of good stories about our family.

~

He always tickles me and calls himself "Mr. Tickle-bickle."

~

Every Saturday we go someplace special.

Dandy

WHEN MY children were very young, our family vacationed in South Florida. In the early evenings before dinner, several older men, all retired and aged seventy-five or so, would gather together to visit and discuss their tennis or golf games. Most of these fellows were well dressed, but one old gent in particular impressed me because he was always impeccably dressed in lime green, canary yellow, or sky blue trousers coordinated with a blazer of equally bright (but contrasting) color as well as matching shirt, socks, etc. He was small and bold and seemed so happy. I never forgot him. Years later, when my wife and I were told we would be first-time grandparents, we were discussing with another couple interesting grandparent names. They told us about a grandfather they knew who was called Dandy. I thought immediately of the happy little dandy in Florida years ago and knew what I wanted to be called. Today my wife and I have six grandchildren whose southern accents have added an extra syllable to my name: Day-Yun-Dy. Music to my ears!

Popeye

MY FATHER is a very strong man. When I first took my children to visit him they were amazed at his big, muscular arms. He would pull his sleeve up and let them touch his muscle. They couldn't believe it! After watching him eat a big salad one night, my son Alexander looked up at me. "Was that spinach he just ate, Daddy? He's just like Popeye!"

It is so funny what kids can put together. Of course Popeye became his name right then.

Now, my kids eat lettuce to get strong like Popeye. (I can't bring myself to tell them that it's not spinach, although sooner or later they will figure it out!) And whenever my kids see the cartoon or hear the song "I'm Popeye the Sailor Man," they immediately think of their very own big, strong Popeye!

The Wisest Thing My Grandfather Ever Said Was . . .

There is no such thing as too much of a good thing.

Gan-Gan

MY TWO sisters and I wondered what our children would call our dad. I believe he really wanted to be called Grandfather. To the firstborn, Chris, came the honor of bestowing "the name." Chris chose Gan-Gan.

As the years passed, six more grandchildren were added, and Dad acquired several more names, including Gigbert, Giggles, and Gig-Gie. I even found myself calling him Gan-Gan or Gig-Gie.

When Dad turned eighty years old he decided he wanted to be called Grandfather, which he thought befitted his status in the family. He was quite adamant about this name change, as only an eighty-year-old father can be. So I dutifully let everyone know his wishes.

Well, he received phone calls and notes from all of the grandchildren, saying, "Gan-Gan, we can't call you Grandfather! You are Gan-Gan," (or Gig-Gie, depending on the favorite name of the different grandchildren). So, with that, my dad remained Gan-Gan and more . . . forever.

D<small>e</small>D<small>e</small>

MY GRANDFATHER was an extraordinary man, loved dearly by all his grandchildren. I'm not sure what first made us call him DeDe. It could be for any of the following reasons:

DeDe was a dedicated fisherman, but he had a degenerative hip disease that gave him a distinctive gait. I remember so well watching him limp to that fishing dock every day. He never let his disease slow him down.

All the people in Paducah, Kentucky, called him Doc. I always assumed it was because that's where they would always expect to find him—on the fishing dock! I found out in later life that it was because he was a dentist. Duh! Isn't it funny that I associated Doc with his love of fishing?

DeDe was also a dandy in his early years. I've seen pictures of him and my grandmother in their younger years. They could have given Clark Gable and Carole Lombard a run for their money! He was so handsome with his hat cocked to one side.

He had a deep love for my grandmother. It was not uncommon for me to walk into their kitchen and see them kissing—

these were my seventy-year-old grandparents! What a wonderful memory I have of their love for each other.

DeDe was also a diehard cook. It did not matter what day of the week it was, he always had us up at 6:00, ready to make us breakfast. He would prepare a feast of sausage links, biscuits, and eggs. He would throw those eggs into the frying pan and then ask us how we wanted them cooked. He would say, "Fried or scrambled?"

My brother and I used to giggle at this. By the time he had asked us, we really did not have much choice. We would just answer "Frambled." Then we would happily eat whatever he put on our plate.

DeDe was dear to me. I miss him deeply. He was the most wonderful grandfather in the world.

One hundred years from now it will not matter what my bank account was, the sort of house I lived in, or the kind of car I drove. . . but the world may be different because I was important in the life of a child.

{The Wisest Thing My Grandfather Ever Said Was . . .}

If you are small you can still be big in heart.

~

If it's worth having, it's worth waiting for.

~

Don't eat too much candy or your teeth will fall out.

~

Never forget those who made a difference in your life.

~

Don't ever judge a book by its cover because
you might miss out on something wonderful.

Pop Pop

MY THREE-YEAR-OLD daughter, Leah, has a very special best buddy. She and I share a bond with this true love in her life. Her buddy is my fifty-three-year old father whom I call Pop. Before she was one year old, Leah gave her favorite playmate and buddy the name Pop Pop. Leah is a child who is blessed with lots of love and attention from an adoring family, but her love for Pop Pop is limitless. She has his full attention and gets continuous affirmations whether she is proudly demonstrating a new ballet step or remembering two-thirds of the words from a song she has heard.

It is possible that Leah sees Pop Pop as a little person much like herself. Not only is he truly a child at heart, but Pop Pop uses a wheelchair, which makes him seem much shorter than he actually stands. Leah has such compassion for Pop Pop and understands that his legs are no longer strong enough to help him walk or run. That doesn't hamper their fun, because Leah is already learning to adapt games and adventures to accommodate

a place for her buddy to roll along beside her, which is just where he wants to be)! With the faith and love of a precious child, she often tells me, "When Pop Pop grows up his legs are gonna be real strong!" That's what true love is all about.

I Love My Grandfather Because . . .

He sits outside with me, and we name the stars.

~

He gives great hugs and sweet sugar kisses.

~

He prays with me.

Gramps

MANY GRANDPARENTS do not like names that insinuate their age. My grandfather was not one of them. He was so proud when I was born that he immediately began calling himself Gramps.

The Gramps character is portrayed in many movies and television shows as a little old man with white or gray hair and tiny glasses on his nose. Well, that was not my grandfather. He was barely fifty-five when I was born, but he acted like he was twenty-five! He had not yet retired. He was very active in tennis and golf (and is still a great golfer). He has always been strong and handsome.

When I was younger, I remember calling out his name, Gramps. He would come limping into the room, acting like Walter Brennan on the *Real McCoys* TV show. He would call out in a funny voice, "What do you want, Little Luke?" I would laugh and laugh.

To this day, my Gramps signifies youthfulness, happiness, and fun to me. He taught me that no matter what your age, you're only as old as you feel! I hope to remember this when I am a Gramps myself.

I Love My Grandfather Because . . .

He helped coach our Little League team.

He comes for my show-and-tell at school so I can show him!

He gave me my first cowboy hat, and he watches westerns with me and tells me about some man named John Wayne.

Paddycake

WHEN MY oldest child, Brian, was a baby, we only saw my parents every few months or so. But whenever we visited, my dad would always put Brian on his lap and play patty-cake with him. It made Brian laugh until he was nearly out of breath. Brian came to expect the patty-cake game with my dad, and he started calling him Granddaddy Patty-cake (now shortened to just Paddycake). He did this to distinguish his two granddaddies.

The name seemed appropriate also because my dad loves to bake, and he sometimes lets Brian help him in the kitchen, now that he is older. Other grandchildren have come along, and they also call this granddad their Paddycake.

My brother recently married. His new wife, wanting to be in on the family lingo, addressed my dad by his nickname. Unfortunately, she didn't remember it quite right and called him Popcorn! We all found it amusing. Now my dad may end up going by either name—which is fine with him!

Big E

M Y FATHER was a great man. He always seemed bigger than life to his four sons and two daughters. He was a man of dignity and integrity, and he was the most honest man I ever knew. He was a proud man and proudest of his family above all. The son of English immigrants, he was always so proper and had the best posture I'd ever seen. "Chin up, shoulders back!" We heard again and again as we were growing up.

When he died, a woman he didn't know came to pay her respects. She said she knew of him as a very visible community leader but also as the man who would tip his hat to her during his regular walks in the park. She had been touched by his gesture of kindness.

When my oldest sister called with the news that she and her husband were expecting the first grandchild, everyone was ecstatic. My mother knew immediately that she would be Nana. Dad, however, was more reserved. He would not hear of being called Grandpa, Gramps, Granddad, or even PaPaw. No, with a name like Ernest F. Leaberry III, he needed a proper title more befitting a man of his stature!

When we were kids, we had a Bill Cosby album that we wore out from playing it so much. One story talked about a father who was referred to by his kids as the Giant. Inspired by Cosby's humor, we referred to Dad as the Giant for years. When he was having such a hard time agreeing to what his grandchild would call him, my sister, who was having the baby, suggested we call him Big E. It was perfect! He liked it, and it stuck.

I am now the proud father of three girls who have already informed my wife and me that when they have children, we shall be known as Big B (my name is Braxton) and Mama T (my wife's name is Teresa). I can only aspire to do as well by my grandchildren as Big E has done by his.

{The Wisest Thing My Grandfather Ever Said Was . . .}

Never drive faster than your angels fly.

Pro

AN AVID golfer's wife grew weary of answering all the midweek phone calls from her husband's golfing buddies wanting to set up tee times for the weekend. Soon she began to answer the phone by saying, "The Pro isn't here...." Both she and her children soon began addressing her husband as Pro.

Upon the arrival of the couple's first grandchild, the question arose, "What shall we teach the child to call him?" Perhaps in a moment of pique, the grandmother suggested Grand Pro. As the grandchild grew and others joined him, this became Babbo. Later that name reverted to Pro. The first great-grandchild interpreted this as Bo. More recently, someone asked why we call him Crow! So Pro—and all of its derivatives—is what my sweet father answers to!

I Love My Grandfather Because . . .

He always has time for me.

Coach

LUTHER PERRIN is my son Tyler's step-great-grandfather. He was born in Louisiana near the small town of Scott. After graduating from college, he returned to teach math at Scott's small high school. He was also the boxing coach, football coach, and both the boys and the girls basketball coach. He would have the boys basketball team on one side of the gym, the girls on the other, and the boxing team in the middle, all practicing at the same time. He has albums full of newspaper write-ups, scores, team pictures, and notes from his players—most addressed to Coach Perrin and all listing the reasons why he was so popular.

When he first came to Nashville, he was introduced to us as Mr. Perrin, but after numerous stories on state championships, hotdog shots on the court, and ninety-five yard touchdown runs, he quickly became Coach.

As soon as Tyler could talk he began calling his grandparents by his chosen names for them. We waited for Mr. Perrin's name to be changed like everyone else's had, but he had a different plan. He loved being Coach and to make sure he stayed Coach, he began reading to Tyler from scrapbooks and helping Tyler make "free throws" into his little Fisher-Price basketball goal. Tyler has heard more coaching stories in four years than any of us have in our whole lives!

One day while shooting free throws in the den, Tyler looked at Mr. Perrin and said, "Coach, shoot it again."

Mr Perrin's face lit up.

At eighty-five years of age, he has been able to reclaim what is to him the most important job in the world, coaching young people!

{The Wisest Thing My Grandfather Ever Said Was . . .}
Anything worth doing is worth doing well.

Uncle Daddy

FOR YEARS, we didn't know that Uncle Daddy was not what all grandchildren called their grandfathers. Believe it or not, my grandmother had her last child one day after her oldest child, Aunt Dot, had her first baby! My Uncle Pat was one day younger than his nephew Tommy!

When Aunt Dot brought little Tommy to meet the family, my Uncle Johnny was introducing the baby around. He said, "This is your Uncle Phil, this is your Uncle Mike, this is your Uncle Pat" (a baby himself!). When he got to my grandfather he said, "And this is your Uncle Daddy!"

All of us grandchildren who came along afterward adopted the name and called our grandfather Uncle Daddy. Of course, our grandmother was Aunt Moma. These names made them feel young—and they really were! They had just had a baby themselves!

Sweet Grandpa

How sweet the sound of Grandpa
When he calls my name to come. . .
As he tells me over and over
That I'm his lovely one.

How sweet the smell of Grandpa
When he comes in from the wind. . .
When he cooks my favorite breakfast
And he treats me like a friend.

How sweet the sight of Grandpa
When I'm acting in my play
Or at the front door of his house
When I go to stay.

How sweet the feel of Grandpa
When he hugs me up real close
Or as he carries me to my bed. . .
These times I treasure most.

My grandpa is felt in my senses
When we're together or when we're apart.
My grandpa is felt deep inside of me,
Way down...in the depths of my heart.

Big Daddy

ONE OF my favorite things to do is to go to the farm with my dad on Saturdays. We cut hay and play on the tractors, and sometimes we just piddle around. My grandfather, who owns the farm, is called "Big Daddy." He is as big and strong as anyone I know. He can toss more hay than my dad, even though he is older.

But Big Daddy is not only big and strong, he has a big heart. When I was a toddler, my parents lived in a house on Big Daddy's property. Not wanting to be the kind of father-in-law who would bug my mom, he kept pretty much to himself. One day my mother was on the phone with my aunt when she heard a noise outside her window.

"Ohmygosh!" she said. "Big Daddy is sitting out behind the house, revving the engine on his four-wheeler."

"What does he want?" my aunt asked my mother.

"That's his way of asking David to come out and play, but he's afraid David is napping so he won't come to the door!" My mom and aunt thought that was so sweet! My mom took me outside, and I rode that four-wheeler all around the farm with my Big Daddy.

We no longer live on his farm, but I see him often because he's always looking for opportunities to baby-sit and teach me all about trucks, tractors, and cows. I know I will always love him in a *big* way—because he is my Big Daddy!

I Love My Grandfather Because . . .

He goes on field trips with me.

He's a doctor, so if I get hurt he knows what to do.

He treats me like a princess.

Obout

MY OBOUT was my special buddy. He wanted me to call him by his name, Robert, but when I was little I couldn't say it. I started with "Obert," and eventually he became "Obout."

I was the first grandchild, and we spent lots of time together. We played out in the yard riding on his lawnmower and working with his flowers. He taught me to love Alabama football. "Roll Tide, Obout!" I would shout. Remember all the pictures of President Kennedy's young son, John, saluting his father's casket? Obout taught me to salute Bear Bryant the same way!

He took me to play golf, and made me my own club—just my size! I never felt that he was too busy for me. He always made me feel very special.

When I had the chicken pox, I stayed with him and Ma-Maw. They pampered me so much! He brought me the biggest bouquet of jonquils you've ever seen from his yard. I'll never forget his beautiful, snow white hair, dark tanned skin (I used to think he was dark because he drank too much coffee), and kind and loving blue eyes.

He passed away on Christmas Eve 1995. The Christmas present I bought him that year summed up my feelings pretty well. It was a sweatshirt. I gave it to him early, and he was able to wear it in the hospital. It read, "Anyone can be a grandfather, but it takes someone special to be OBOUT!" He was truly unique and special. I miss him very much.

Pawp

MY GRANDSON'S name is David, and he is named after me, his PawPaw. I am known for shortening the names of everyone in my family. For instance, I call my granddaughter Jessica, Jess, my daughter Gina, Gin, and my son-in-law Battle, Bat.

One day, I was sitting in my den, and David walked in, acting very big and tough for a three-year-old. "Well, hi, David!" I said as he marched through the room.

"Hi, Pawp!" he said nonchalantly back to me. I loved it! He had shortened my name just like I do everyone else's.

I have six grandchildren—five who call me Paw Paw and one who calls me Pawp. He is so precious to me. I guess he's a chip off the old block, not only in name, but in other ways as well.

The Wisest Thing My Grandfather Ever Said Was . . .

Read the directions before you put stuff together.

Da–Daddy

O N A farm in Tennessee lives J. C. Gillentine, a big, rugged man who runs a Christian Camp for churches throughout the state. The camp is situated on many acres and overlooks a beautiful lake. If you visit the camp, you may see J. C. pitching hay, loading trees, or keeping up the land. But if you catch him on the right day, you might also see him playing Barbies, marbles, or horsie-ride with his three granddaughters, Caitlin (he calls her CD), Mariah (he calls her the Wind), and MacKinzie (he calls her Mac). They call him Da-Daddy, and to them Da-Daddy is a big, huggable teddy bear.

And on special occasions, you may also catch Da-Daddy on the back deck, surrounded by those three precious little girls, showing them the beauty of the lake, the wonder of nature, and the majesty of God.

Grumpa

I CALLED my grandpa Grandpa until I was a teenager. He is a very big man with a very loud voice. He has a way of letting us know what he wants exactly when he wants it. He could order us around with only one word uttered because his voice used to scare us to death!

When I was older, I had a talk with my mother. We are a very quiet family and rarely ever raise our voices. It was unnerving for me to visit my grandparents' house. My Grandpa was not mean; he just frightened me with his method of communication. My mother explained to me that that was just the way he talked. He sounded grumpy all the time, but he wasn't. She explained to me that he was probably hard of hearing (which he would never admit) and that caused his voice to come out as blaring as it did.

The next time I was visiting, my grandfather called out to me from the den, where he sat with the television turned up to almost the maximum level. I couldn't come at that moment but that didn't stop him from yelling my name over and over again until I came into the room. "What do you want, Grumpa?" I asked, frustrated, as I walked into the den.

"What did you call me?" he looked up at me with a half grin on his face.

"Grumpa," I said, looking down, trying not to laugh from my nervousness.

He began to laugh the loudest laugh I have ever heard. "Well, you come here and see Grumpa and tell me how you've been doing."

I went over and sat beside him. It was then that I realized how much I truly loved him and that his bark was much bigger than his bite! Since then I've called him Grumpa. Believe it or not, it is a special, affectionate name between only the two of us.

Children's children are a crown to the aged.

—PROVERBS 17:6

Daddy Doc

WE HAD the choice of calling my grandfather Daddy Horace or Daddy Melvin, because his name is Horace Melvin.

In a town as small as half a minute and with as many animals as humans, my grandfather was the makeshift veterinarian. Whenever a pig lost its squeal or a chicken was cooped up, the neighbors called on "Doc" Copley. Daddy Doc probably delivered more calves and colts than a real vet could ever imagine—and all without a lick of schooling. He also had his own homemade anesthetic!

So when it came time to choose a name for him, instead of Daddy Horace or Daddy Melvin, we called him Daddy Doc. For some reason, he preferred that over Horace or Melvin!

{The Wisest Thing My Grandfather Ever Said Was ...}

If it is to be, it is up to me.

Honor

WHEN OUR first grandchild was due, it seemed reasonable to give some thought to what name each grandparent wanted to be called. Because this grandchild was going to have step-grandparents, he or she would have more than the usual number of grandparents, and it was very important that they each have their own names.

One day my husband and I were walking in the park with our two daughters. They were excited about becoming first-time aunts and asked their dad if he had decided what he wanted to be called. Without missing a step and with a twinkle in his eye, he said, "Your Honor." My husband is a circuit court judge. We thought the name fit, and so did my grandson.

Today, two years later, our grandson does call his grandfather Honor. It is an honorable name for an honorable man!

Big Big

WHEN MY grandson Drew began to talk he called his grandfather Big Big. To a little one-year-old looking up at his six-foot-two-inch grandfather, my husband was mighty big to him! If you could see Big Big with Drew, you would understand why he holds such a big place in Drew's heart.

Big Big and Drew have a very close relationship. They go camping in the mountains, play ball, and Big Big even helps with fund-raisers at the school Drew attends. Drew takes great pride in Big Big and one day asked him to come visit his school. He apparently had told all the kids that Big Big was coming to see him. When one child asked, "Who is Big Big?" Drew responded "Just you wait until you see him!"

Each one of our grandchildren gets to come separately to our house to stay on weekends. This makes it a special time for each one, with just the grandchild and Gran and Big Big. My husband began a ritual that became a tradition. On these weekends, he walks into the room where I am and says "Gran, I need to run a few errands."

This is the signal to whichever child is with us that he or she gets to go with Big Big and he will buy them a very special treat.

We didn't realize this tradition was starting until the day, on Drew's special weekend, when he said to my husband, "Big Big, don't we need to run some errands?"

My husband and I just looked at each other and smiled. Now errands are very special bonding trips Big Big takes with each grandchild.

I Love My Grandfather Because . . .

He always says, "You can do it! Just try!"

I feel so safe when he is around.

Skinny

OUR GRANDFATHER was known as a very distinguished man. Employed by Western Union, he became so proficient at Morse Code that he was one of the very few who could send it speedily. Once he even traveled with a US president to The Greenbriar in West Virginia to send ticker tape reports. We used to listen to his stories in amazement. Our grandfather was so cool!

We grandchildren called him Skinny, but not because he was thin, although he was. It was much simpler than that. His family and friends would called him Kenny, short for Kenneth, but as children, we were unable to pronounce Kenny; it came out "Skinny." The nickname stuck! Throughout our entire lives everyone called him by that name. Even his wife eventually referred to him as Skinny or Skin.

He took to the name quite well. He was full of fun and always joking with us. In later years he used to sit in front of the television set with us, pointing out funny things in the Benny Hill skits that we were watching. We got quite a kick out

of this. His eyes were always dancing. He was a wonderful grandfather and we, his grandchildren and great-grandchildren, loved him dearly.

PaPa

W HEN WE learned our first grandchild was on the way, Linn, my wife, named herself Gran. That was settled. Gran was the perfect name for her; it suited her to a T.

But what about me? What fit me best? What sounded right to go along with Gran?

For months we tried to settle on a perfect grandfather name. Eventually, we came up with Granddad. It sounded good with Gran-Gran and Granddad. But we weren't convinced it was right.

Finally the big day arrived. Our daughter Becky was in labor. Aubrey Sara was on the way! As we stayed in the waiting room with our son-in-law, Phil, pacing the floor and praying for a safe delivery, all of a sudden a lightbulb turned on inside of my head! It was June 21—my own deceased grandfather's birthday. He was a fine and stately gentleman—a college president revered by everyone—and all his children and grandchildren had called him PaPa.

"That's it," I said. "Aubrey is being born on PaPa's birthday. I shall be called PaPa!"

And so we became PaPa 'n' Gran. I love to hear Aubrey and Davis call me PaPa. It links me to my past and brings back such fond memories. However, I admit that once in a while when they call me Pops or Poppy as a term of endearment, that's when I truly melt.

{The Wisest Thing My Grandfather Ever Said Was . . .}

Always be yourself, because no one will ever love you deeply if they don't know the real you.

~

Don't take life too seriously.

Diddley

DIDDLEY WAS the most special grandfather in the world. He was given his name by my younger brother, Jim. Jim tried to say "Granddaddy," but it just came out Diddley. So that's what we all called him.

He was the kind of grandfather who would buy two large pizzas for the two of us just to be sure we had enough! He would find out where I was baby-sitting and come walk around the house late at night to make sure I was OK. He took me and my brother fishing anytime we wanted to go. Once, we accidentally let all of the crickets go from the bait holder into the boat. All two hundred of them! Diddley didn't get mad! He made it a fun day, one that we'll never forget.

My brother and I knew how much he loved us. He was always there for us. At any event we participated in he was there cheering us on.

Our family's backyard connected with Diddley's, and we crossed back and forth going to see him so many times that our little feet beat down a path from our house to his. Today when I see that path I am filled with many emotions—happiness and love as the warm memories flood my heart, joy and thanksgiving that I was so fortunate to have had Diddley as my grandfather, and sadness because I miss him more than words can say.

{The Wisest Thing My Grandfather Ever Said Was . . .}

Remember your past with your present—
write it down and never forget to tell it to your children.

Success is happiness, not money.

Don't try to grow up too fast.

Boddy

T HE TENNESSE State Fair of 1945 was held in my hometown. Back then it was not customary for schools to let students out of class to attend such events without a note from the parents. A creative set of twins, Billy and Bobby, along with a neighborhood friend, decided to play hooky and go to the fair without their parents' consent. These three little fourth-graders were not going to let their lack of a note from their parents stand in the way of a day filled with rides, shows, and cotton candy! They conjured up a very creative plan—they thought. The friend wrote a note that said, "Please let Billy and Boddy [instead of Bobby] out of school to go to the fair. Thank you, Mrs. Beulah Teal."

The boys failed to proofread the note, and the first draft was turned in to their teacher. Needless to say, the teacher caught the misspelling, and they did not get to attend the fair that day. From then on, Billy adopted the nickname Boddy for his twin brother.

Years passed, and Bobby's grandchildren were coming along. He did not want to be called Grandfather or Granddaddy. During this time of decision, he related the state fair story to us. We chose Grandboddy as his grandfather name, which the grandchildren have now shortened to just Boddy.

I Love My Grandfather Because . . .

When my parents divorced, he helped me understand it was not my fault.

~

He pushes me high as the sky on my swing.

~

He is always there for me.

Kookyfoo

THE NAME Kookyfoo came about in the games that Bob Whitaker played with his grandchildren, in which an imaginary language was spoken to describe people and events—much akin to the phonetic, but artificial language entertainer Sid Caesar used in his television skits.

Young children have vivid imaginations that lead to exciting adventures if you enter into their world at their level. Kookyfoo did just that, unlocking the door to that world where the only limit is the extent of one's own imagination and where a special language becomes the vehicle to travel to the farthest frontiers. Porch swings were transformed into space vehicles to take everyone to the edge of the solar system, "where Pluto wagged its tail," "a sea monster swam and reared its head on Neptune," and the "Milky Way was an ice cream shop."

As the grandchildren (ages seven through fourteen), accompanied their grandfather on one of these imaginary adventures, the conversation between them and Granddad took on the form of "crazy talk"—languages that could sound like a mixture of

Chinese, Russian, German, etc. Kookyfoo came out as a name for
a particular grandchild traveling the stars with Granddad at that
moment. The others were so tickled over the name that they
began turning it back on their grandfather!

"Who's Kookyfoo?" Granddad Bob would say when greeting
one of the children. They quickly learned to respond "*You* are!"

Dat

WHEN MY daughter was born, my father, who lives in another state, jumped on a plane and arrived in time to be one of the first persons to hold her. He stayed through the week and rarely moved from the rocking chair in the den, where he held his new grandaughter and sang to her for hours.

After he left, I worried that the distance between our homes would make it difficult for him to have a close relationship with our little Lauren. We visited him twice during her first year, and then I became pregnant with my second child, making it difficult for us to make the long trip.

Lauren was nineteen months old before my father was able to come and visit us again. Enthusiastically, I told her again and again that her grandfather was coming to visit, hoping she would love him as I do. When he arrived, Lauren greeted him as if she knew quite well that this was a special person in her life. We went out to eat dinner, and she sat next to him, studying him closely.

Back at home, it was Lauren's bedtime. I asked her to tell her granddad good night. She walked over to him on her way to her room, stopped in front of him, and stood silently for a few seconds. She then gave a big smile and a wave and said, "Bye Dat!" So, "Dat was Dat," as they say. Theirs has been a close, loving, special relationship despite my worries about the long distance between them.

The Wisest Thing My Grandfather Ever Said Was . . .

Graduate. Go on to college.
Never, never stop learning good things.

If it sounds too good to be true, it probably is.

*The authors extend their sincere gratitude to the
following individuals who contributed to this book.
(Stories were edited for clarity and style.)*

Jane Alvis	*Tressa Copley*	*Donna Gillentine*
Tracey Anderson	*Helen Costa*	*Lisa Gorman*
Patsy Baccus	*Cara Crews*	*Adonis Gordon*
Floyd Barrett	*Carolyn Culpepper*	*Mary Griffin*
Holly Baulch	*Karen Davies*	*Shirley Hannah*
Lemelia Bonner	*Sandy Davis*	*Gayle Moyer Harris*
Shirley Bornstein	*Angela Dixon*	*Mildred Henderson*
Brenda Bradford	*Andy Dixon*	*Carrie Henry*
Jim Bradford	*Vicki Dooley*	*Becky Henry*
Sandy Brewington	*Lynn Dorris*	*Tracy Henry*
Jackie Brown	*Vonda Dunn*	*Kathy Hill*
Vicki Brown	*Lois Ellis*	*DeeAnn Hodge*
Beth Burress	*Luanna Elrod*	*Sally Hudgins*
Taylor Cawley	*Ashley Evans*	*Sandy Hudson*
Sheila Clark	*Darlene Evans*	*Brenna Isaacs*
Gary Clark	*Linda Evans*	*Patricia Jacob*
Shirley Clary	*Karen Ford*	*Andra Jenkins*
Paulette Coleman	*Cindy Fowler*	*Montez Jenkins*
Sherri Cook	*Gina Frey*	*Lannie Jewell*

Marj Kathmann
Pat Kepler
E. Braxton Leaberry
Jerry Lemons
Dell Lewis
Robbie Malone
Ashley Mankins
Debbie Maples
Neal Matthews
Sydney Myers
Jean Oldfield
Ashleigh Orme
Cathy Overby
Battle Page
Gina Page

Colette Patterson
Micki Pendleton
Frank Pendleton
Carole Pettus
Alan Powell
Marinda Rice
Bob Richter
Peggy Robinson
Angie Ryan
Jennifer Scott
Jonathan Seyfred
Kathy Steakley
William Stevenson
Lori Steward
Deatrice Swett

Heidi Taylor
Sherrie Teal
Keith Thetford
Carmel Trevathan
Donna
VanDoorninck
Julia Webb
Pam Wells
Robert Whitaker
Glenda Whitaker
Amber White
Benja Whitelaw
Pamela York

*If you have any stories you'd like to share about your
grandmothers, grandfathers, or grandchildren, please write to us.*
C. Booth/M. Henderson
P. O. Box 50173
Nashville, Tennessee 37205

Index of Grandfathers